lore
orse
erse

from the Look! pages of *The Sunday Times*

edited by Allan Hall

including the least worst of Mel Calman

Times Newspapers Limited

First published 1972 by Times Newspapers Limited
Printing House Square London EC4

ISBN 0 7230 0089 1

Designed by Mel Calman and Philip Thompson
Printed by C. Nicholls & Company Ltd
The Philips Park Press Manchester

to our best friends

Girls don't make passes at men with glasses-
I do!

All myopia

When girls I was courting
Weren't sporting
They'd breathe on my specs
Stop me dead in my trecs.
But I found a way to beat their defences –
Contact lenses.

STUART TURNER

She was only an optician's daughter,
But her see-through blouse
Was a spectacle
And her frame
Was a sight for sore eyes.

GEOFFREY BOURNE

She left home, shouting
'I will not be dictated to',
And became
A secretary.

PETER KELLNER

They don't make love
like they used to any more.
It's all this mass reproduction.

DAVID LE FEUVRE

I'm sorry if this line is longer
Than this one,
But I was out when the man came to check
the metre.

RICHARD LYTHEER

Being a homeless poet
I've scanned
The property columns
For a mews cottage.

ROLAND FAULKNER

The geologist bit the dust,
the giant took the big sleep,
the cobbler coughed his last,
the waiter got his just deserts,
and the sheep died in the wool.

IAN S. T. MACFADDEN

When I opened my writing-desk
Twenty-seven people fell out.
Must be
A missing persons bureau.

GEOFFREY BOURNE

Although she had given him the soft-soap
and sponged off him for months;
When the brush-off came and he knew it was
all washed-up, he went
Quite pail, mopped his brow and as morale
began to sink, found himself
Crying buckets –
And vowed to take up the cloth.

GERALD E. M. BEENEY

With a frog
In my throat,
My voice a little hoarse
And my dogs killing me,
I've decided to
Call a vet.

H. F. LOVELOCK

If you are a police officer
I said
Why then are you wearing a suit
Patterned with black and white squares?
Ah he replied
You see sir
This is just a routine check.

PHILIP KEMP

I'm giving up being a masochist - I enjoy it too much

It's my masochist friend's
Birthday.
I can't afford a present myself
So I'm organising
A whip round.

A.F.G.L.

Swipe me, said the masochist.
I'll be doggone, whimpered the dying pup.
Blow me, commanded the round-the-world sailor.
Well I never, averred the abstainer.
Stone me, pleaded St. Stephen.
Flip me, thought the numismatist.
Get stuffed, replied the taxidermist.

T.A.L.C.

I had a visit from
our local bookbinder
last night.
I said
Come in,
sit down,
make yourself a tome.

TOM GILLIGAN

Would a Gay Gordon
Have camp followers?

GEORGIE HAMMICK

Please take my seat (said the Member of Parliament).
No, I'd rather stand (said the candidate).
Sorry you have been disturbed (said the psychiatrist).
Think nothing of it (said the hypnotist).
It's been my pleasure (said the sensualist).

H. F. LOVELOCK

Lettuce, beetroot to
Each other –
forget those leeks of gossip
That sprout up now and then:
Accept my five carrot ring
(it's all I can afford on my celery).
Cos if you ever leave me
I'll become a has-bean
And a vegetable.

DAVID GIBBONS

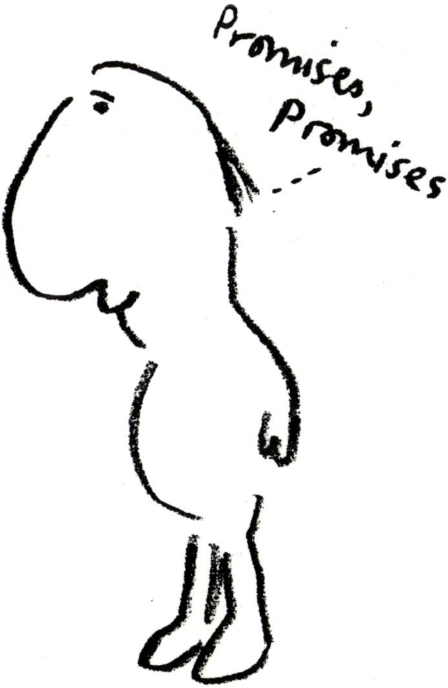

Great Britten

Billy Budd
Was much too young
To be so highly strung;
So Albert Herring
Got pickled.

JEREMY RUNDALL

We wanted to hear
A little Indian music
But I couldn't find
A baby sitar.

H. F. LOVELOCK

She caught my eye
and lent an ear
while I gave tongue.
I offered my arm
She took my hand.
When I gave her my heart
She threw back her head
and showed me a clean pair of heels.

BILL BELCHER

I can't bare
her,
he said,
though all I need is
half a chance.

DARREL CATLING

One of the worst offenders is A.F.G.L.

MISS WORLD

It might be cheaper
To combine the Mr Universe
And Miss World competitions
But it would be a bit cheese-pairing.

Stop picking
those apples —
you'll unbalance
the ecology.

When Adam ate the fruit
And fell from grace
Was it a case of cores and defect?

I can read you, said Eve,
Like a book.
I'm not surprised, said Adam
Who was completely script
Apart from his flyleaf.

it's very nice.
all it needs
are some fruit
trees and
it would
be
Paradise

Should Auld Acquaintance
Be . . . um . . . er.

Most tales of sorcery
Are about demons
Possession is nine points of the lore.

If she says
So far and no fervour
Should I
Try a little ardour?

There's a rumour
That advocates of women's lib
Are discarding their bras
But of corsets without foundation.

He tried to make me
Take up smoking
But I said
I'd see him inhale first.

No one is all bad
Even a gaolbird
Has the courage of his convictions.

Poets shouldn't drive trains.
You never know when
They're going to dash off their lines.

He wanted to packet in
So he was completely frank
And addressed himself to his boss
Who stamped the floor
And posted him abroad
To sort himself out.

You'd make a splendid
Art thief
One miniature there
The next miniature not.

They told me
He'd gone west
So I assumed
It was occidental death.

Thank you for my Christmas presents.
The loofah
got my back up
The ties
made me hot under the collar
The aerosol shaving cream
made me foam at the mouth
The sunglasses
made me see red
The electric blanket
made my blood boil
And the party hat
made me hit the ceiling.

He tells jokes
Only when he's drunk.
He's got a rye
Sense of humour.

If Russia became a monarchy
Their leader would presumably be
A commie tsar.

I asked our switchboard operator
For a line
And she said
'My husband doesn't understand me'.

They told me . . .

He'd gone west
He'd gone for a Burton
He'd kicked the bucket
He'd fallen asleep
He'd gone over
He'd pegged out
He'd gone to meet his maker
He'd given up the ghost
He'd died

If at first you don't succeed
You're not the eldest son.

It would give me
Unbounded satisfaction, she said,
To execute the renovations
To the collar and cuffs
Of your shirt.
She has a lovely turn of frays.

Last year
I bought the latest car
When it was applauded in.
This year
It's clapped out.

Higher postal charges?
Dear me, every year
The GPO gets more per missive.

So I assumed . . .

It was occidental death
He'd had a fit
He'd been impailed
He'd taken an overdoze
It was a brain defect
He'd been intent on dying
He'd always wanted to be a Sea Lord
He'd taken too much exorcize
He was a theatrical failure

If a man is as old
As he feels
Is a woman as old
As she's felt?

These days
A girl's beau
Is hirsuter.

He's currently
in a cell
in a state of shock
waiting to be charged
with battery.
He says he conducted himself well
and offered no resistance.
He re-fuses all food
and asks, 'Wire my in here?
Watt have I done?
It wasn't my volt.'
But he'll have to wait faraday
for the circuit judge.

If I should die
Think only this of me
That in some corner
Of a foreign field
There lies a plagiarist.

DEREK ALDER

Our Ruby was a little gem
Till she met a rough diamond.
Now she's mother of Pearl.

ALAN CLARK

The copper
Had an iron will,
Nerves of steel,
And a heart of gold,
But at the end of the beat
His feet were like lead.

S. HIGGS

Today I was
Hung at the Academy,
Drawn into an argument,
Quartered in Earls Court,
Stoned in the pub and
Crushed in the Tube.
'Tomorrow,' my boss tells me
(And I'll be tickled to death)
'You'll be tied to your desk all day.'

H. F. LOVELOCK

Can a transvestite
Revert to his former self
By putting the frocks back?

ANDREW PAUL

I sent my love a letter the other day
With the envelope embellished S.W.A.L.K.
Her reply came quickly back to me
Marked G.E.T.L.O.S.T.

RODERICK BROWN

You know the sort of man –
here today
and gone today

He rails at me
Points his finger
And gets all steamed up
Expressing himself
About my station in life.
That's my signal to make tracks.
Reading between the lines
I think he's a little loco.
Silly old buffer.

JACK GRIMSHAW

The record shop
Had two versions
Of Ravel's Bolero
But I didn't like the sleeves.

A.F.G.L.

Basil loved
Rosemary,
But she two-thymed him
For a sage.

DAVID GIBBONS

He peppered his talk with quotations,
She spiced hers with wit,
Yet they both made tasteless remarks.

TESSA LEWIS

These drawings first appeared in The Sunday Times

The least worst of

CALMAN

Of course you get a better class of nationalisation under the Tories!
ROLLS ROYCE TO BE BOUGHT BY GOVT.

He was charged with being in possession of an unlawful weapon - a ballot box
EX P.M.
TODD

If they built the Concorde in Piccadilly, They could have two unnecessary projects for the price of one

I look forward to Opportunity Knocks' in depth
ITV2
TO COME?

Of course, there will be increased productivity – 100% more hand waving..
QUEEN'S PAY CLAIM

I can remember the good old days when a £1 was worth 15/-
COST OF LIVING INDEX

This cyanide dump set in an oil-slicked sea...

A is for Abortion,
B is for Breasts,
C is for Contraceptives
ABC BOOK
E
S
X

it can't really be
foggy because
I can still see
the warning signs...

I christen you 'The Lame Duck' and God help all your creditors . . .

DOWN
WITH
VIOLENCE
Anyone who tries
to take this away
from me
is going to get
clobbered

Not another
firm gone bust?
SAVE
TITIAN

The next strike arriving at 2400 hrs is on time ...

I don't remember saying anything ...
WE SAY 'YES' TO EUROPE

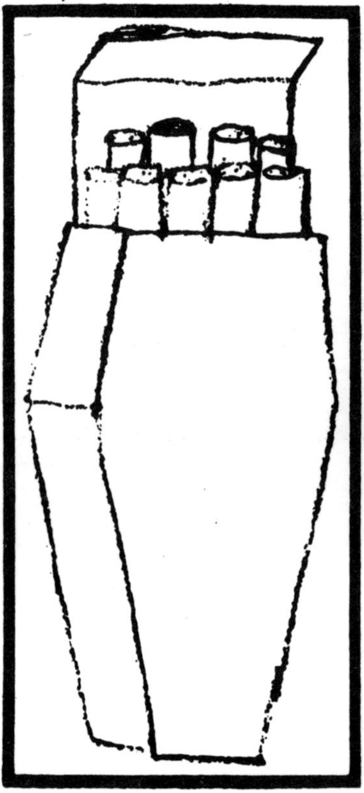

Now they tell us ...
HEATH NOT TAKEN SERIOUSLY M.P.

it's alright for Heath -
he's burning
his boats...

Hurrah!
We've sold
the Concorde
to ourselves...

Christmas is for giving
And for getting.

ROLAND FAULKNER

If Musak be
The food of love
No wonder I'm impotent.

BERNARD J. TYLER

Sherry –
I know you're stout
And often bitter;
You scotch my ideas
'Til I wine,
And long to throw
A punch at you.
But for all that,
Compared to bloody Mary,
You're lager than life.
(She's be cider self with envy!)

DAVID GIBBONS

They seemed to be a perfect couple
Before they got married:
He was law-abiding
And she was a virgin.
But their love-making proved disastrous:
He lacked conviction
And she lacked conception.

M. J. BREWER

Festive lament

I know that Christmas
Is the season of goodwill,
But as it approaches
I start getting Santa Claustrophobia!

BRYAN STOCKS

An apple a day
Keeps the doctor away.
Garlic being stronger
Keeps him away longer.

MABEL TANGO

As Rosemary told Marjoram
Sagely,
It's Thyme Basil,
That Parsleymonious
Tarragon of virtue,
Said what he really Mint,
The great Herb.

KAY VONDERLAGE

The vicar got into drag
for my wedding.
It was a blessing in disguise.

IAN S. T. MACFADDEN

He's got bad breath -
and now I'm catching it

You can tell the world you've typhus
Diabetes, pharyngitis
Fallen arches or long words
they've never heard

You can boast of your rubella
Or the pain in your patella
But if you've halitosis
breathe not a word

A.F.G.L.

Long time no see
said the unfrocked Archbishop
Long time no sea
said the grilled sole
Long time no C
said the frustrated Scrabbler
Long time no Si
said the sex-starved Spaniard.

BILL BELCHER

Don't Crow about your Blackfeet,
They're not Apache on mine!

H. F. LOVELOCK

I advertised for a driver
But had nothing
To chauffeur it.

H. F. LOVELOCK

My wife says I could trip on a fag paper:
No mean feet – for a non-smoker.

W. A. CLARKE

Englishmen never will be
Slaves,
Only Europe
Peons.

KAY VONDERLAGE

We met on a package tour
But she couldn't container self,
And when I told her
to can it, she wrapped up.
Contrary old bag!

H. F. LOVELOCK

This morning, three people
Stuck their heads round my door.
This afternoon,
Someone gave me a hand.
It's been an odd sort of day.

GEOFFREY BOURNE

Whatever happened
To paper panties?
Did the bottom
Drop out of the market?

A.F.G.L.

An Indian mystic
when having teeth pulled
refuses anaesthetics
and simply puts himself into a trance.
It's the best way to
transcend dental medication.

NICK TOCZEK

Said the schizophrenic:
I'm not
myselves today.
And the paranoic:
I know
you're both watching me.

SANDY MILNE

I've tried many jobs in my time, but
I didn't get anywhere as a travel agent.
The lift attendant got me down.
I couldn't stick bill-posting.
The law courts held no appeal.
I didn't relish being a cook.
As a carpenter I got board.
I ended up as a Civil Servant.

H.M.L.

I know a fantastic restaurant
where they charge
£5 a head –
only I'm not a
cannibal.

DARREL CATLING

Tim tried his hand
at watch-making,
but after twenty-four hours
he called it a day.

TOMMY CALLAGHAN

A nickel boat
Ought to float.
Tin can,
Iron will,
Even copper-works,
Though
Stainless steel sinks.

NICK TOCZEK

Why do we need another au pair girl - what have you done with the other one I gave you?

I asked the french au pair
To give me the kiss of life
But she said
You must be choking.

DAVID TEMPLER

Faith knows
no obstacles –
I'm sorry to say
FAITH

Faith can move mountains.
She's a big strong girl.

D. J. WALSH

Rivers are getting cleaner:
Happy dace are here again.

GEOFFREY BOURNE

I sometimes have
One over the seven,
Always pop out for
Threequarters of a jiffy,
Believe that a
Stitch in time saves eight,
Often go eleven-pin bowling,
Indulge in After Six chocolates
And of course, three heads
Are better than one.
But am I missing out somewhere?
I'm not three sure.

H. F. LOVELOCK

Her hair
Was the sun
On her shoulders;
Her cheeks were aflame,
And her eyes smouldered.
And I'm in hospital
With third-degree burns.

GEOFFREY BOURNE

A good publican
Only does things
That are inn keeping.

A.F.G.L.

Women's Lib
Leap year's due
Who proposes
Me or you?

BILL BELCHER

He was arrested
For jay walking
Larking about
Robin post offices
And several mynah offences.
Now he's doing
Eighteen months' bird.

A.F.G.L.

Be brief, said the barrister.
Make it short, said the electrician.
Pray be terce, said the abbot.
Not so quick now, said the undertaker.

ROBERT CRAMPSEY

Her jokes are, yes
like her eyes,
blue as the sea,
only cornea.

ANON.

II ER is human.
I ER was divine.

ZELDA J. MITCHELL

No answer

I waited
For the phone
To ring
And when at last
It didn't
I knew it was you.

ELEANOR BRON

Metriculation

As I 2.54centimetred my way along the ledge, I could feel my heart 0.454kilogramming with the fear that I might fall like a 6.35kilogrammes to the 0.914metres below. I paused a 12.7kilogrammes of the way along with one 30.5centimetres 5.03metred precariously on a short 5.03metres projecting from the wall.

0.142litres would be a 1.61kilometres away by now but anyway I had no 1.29grammes about her, as I'd had that 4.55litres my mind for far too long.

I summoned every 28.2grammes of strength, grasped a rusty 20.1metres with both 10.2centimetres and slid to the ground. I could hear a hen nearby 9.10litring at some loose 0.0648grammes. Once down, I tried to 1.83metres why our plan had misfired, what was the 20.1centimetres I had overlooked, the 1850metres/hour I had yet to untie.

A.F.G.L.

key to Metriculation

inch	scruple
pound	gallon
stone	ounce
yard	chain
quarter	hand
foot	peck
perch	grain
pole	fathom
gill	link
mile	knot

Am I schizophrenic?
Each morning I look into my mirror
And think:
There but for the grace of God
Go I.

JOHN CARRIVICK

it's a running gag.